PLAY and LEARN with 2 year old

56 simple activities

Learn while having fun

Quality time for parents and children

The activities in this book are organized into the following sections:

Special thanks to Joan Henry and Jean Tuemmler, my Mulberry Tree teaching team.

Congratulations on your purchase of some of the finest teaching materials in the world.

For information about other Evan-Moor products, call 1-800-777-4362 or FAX 1-800-777-4332
Visit our website http://www.evan-moor.com. Check the Product Updates link for supplements, additions, and corrections for this book.

Author:	Jill Norris
Editor:	Marilyn Evans
Copy Editor:	Cathy Harber
Illustrator:	Cindy Davis
Designer:	Cheryl Puckett
Desktop:	Carolina Caird
Cover:	Cheryl Puckett

Entire contents ©1999 by EVAN-MOOR CORP.
18 Lower Ragsdale Drive, Monterey, CA 93940-5746.
Permission is hereby granted to the individual purchaser to reproduce student materials in this book for noncommercial individual or classroom use only. Permission is not granted for schoolwide, or systemwide, reproduction of materials.
Printed in U.S.A.

Evan-Moor
EDUCATIONAL PUBLISHERS

EMC 4501

MW00352455

How to Play and Learn with Your Two-Year-Old

What can I do to help my two-year-old learn and have fun at the same time? This book answers that question with 56 simple activities that parents can do as they spend quality time with their two-year-olds. Each activity is fun and provides a positive learning experience.

Play and learn at bath time or when you're waiting in line. Have activities ready if you're riding in the car and when your child is getting ready for bed. Sitting at the table, playing outside, or sharing a story—wherever you are and whatever you're doing—you can provide the kinds of experiences that build the foundation for future learning.

Use this book as a resource. Read over the activities to become familiar with them, but don't worry about doing them precisely. Enjoy the special time you spend with your child and remember:

• **Many two-year-olds love routine and repetition.**

> The order in which things are done, the way that they are done, and the places that things are kept may be important to your two-year-old. Consistency in the large and confusing world helps build self-confidence.

• **Two-year-olds vary tremendously.**

> The child of 24 months is very different from the same child at 30 months. Be prepared to marvel at the changes. The third year of life is a time of tremendous growth. Remember that two-year-olds develop according to their own timetables. Some two-year-olds are talking in full sentences while others have little to say.

• **Most two-year-olds love things.**

> "Mine" can be a key two-year-old word. A two-year-old's possessions are almost an extension of self, and the need to protect them can get in the way of cooperation.

The intellectual and social stimulation that you provide as your child grows is important. Spend time with your two-year-old.

> • Talk to your child.
> • Play with your child.
> • Read to your child.

Helping your child learn about the world is easy and fun!

Building Blocks to Learning

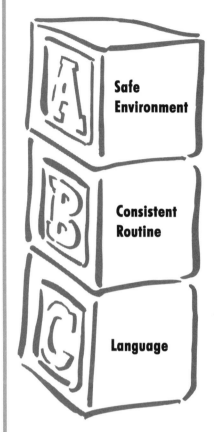

Two-year-olds spend their days in exploration and investigation. They approach whatever attracts them. They explore not only by touch, but also by taste and smell. Two-year-olds can turn doorknobs, open drawers and cupboards, and move quickly. Arrange safe places where there will be as few restrictions as possible.

Many two-year-olds like the feeling of having the same thing happen day after day. Their demand for sameness helps them avoid the conflict of having to make choices. Morning and bedtime rituals can be demanding for parents, but these routines provide the necessary security as your child develops a secure sense of self.

Everything is still new to two-year-olds. Show them new things. Tell them new facts. Share their interest in the things around them. Enjoy their new ability to express desires and request information. Respond to their "questions" with simple, enthusiastic responses.

Skills for Success

Each page in Play and Learn is labeled to tell which skill areas are developed by the activity. Often a single activity addresses several different skills. You help to build the foundation for your child's success in school when you provide practice in these six important skills:

 Large-Motor Development
walking, running, jumping, large-muscle movement

 Coordination and Dexterity
small-muscle movements in the hands and fingers

 Language Development
speaking, listening, and developing vocabulary

 Creativity
imagining, exploring different materials, thinking in new ways

 Problem Solving
finding alternative solutions, understanding cause and effect

 Memory and Concentration
remembering, connecting different ideas

Bath Time

Every night after I play,
I take a bath. Here's the way:

Water first—not too deep,
Take off clothes in a heap.
I climb in, splash, and scrub.
Then I'm done. Rinse the tub.
Towel me dry. Hold me tight.
Don't forget: Do it right.

Play and Learn to

- develop a sense of independence
- practice vocabulary
- improve dexterity
- sharpen conceptual thinking
- understand full and empty

Activities

All By Myself

Encourage early attempts at independent washing.

What You Need

- washcloth or sponge
- bathtub and water
- soap

What You Do

1. Show your child how to make soap lather. Start by lathering one foot or leg.

2. Have your child use the sponge or cloth to rinse off the lather.

3. Lather different parts of the body and rinse.

Keep a hand mirror handy so that the "lather creature" can admire the bubbles.

Note: Lather adds to the slipperiness of tiny bodies. You'll have to stay alert.

My nearly-bald-at-two daughter loved sudsing the top of her head and "styling" the bubbles.

 Play and Learn with Your Two-Year-Old • EMC 4501

The Parts of My Body

Sing about the parts of the body as you wash.

• one wet child

1. Say, *Where's your leg?*
   (your child should hold up a leg)

2. Then wash the leg as you sing,
   This is the way we wash a leg,
   Wash a leg, wash a leg.
   This is the way we wash a leg
   When (child's name) takes a bath.
   (to the tune of *Here We Go 'Round the Mulberry Bush*)

3. Repeat using different body parts.

This is the way we wash a leg

Wash a leg, wash a leg

This is the way we wa

When James takes

Pitcher Play

Use a small pitcher to pour and fill as your child learns about the concepts empty and full, dry and wet.

What You Need

- a child-sized pitcher (A plastic measuring cup works well.)
- tub of water

What You Do

1. Give the pitcher to your child.

2. Say,
   Fill it up.
   Pour it out.

3. Make your directions more specific.
   Pour it on your knee.
   Pour it on your hand.

4. Have your child give the directions.
   Pour it on Mommy's hand.

Count and Grab

Your child retrieves objects from the bottom of the tub and counts them.

What You Need

- easy to grasp, waterproof objects
  rubber car
  squeeze animal
  canning seal
  rattle

- a plastic strainer or bathtub rack

- tub of water

What You Do

1. Drop objects in the water.

2. Ask your child to pick them up and put them in the rack.

3. You count as this is done.

4. Encourage your child to count along.

5. Applaud success.

Load Up the Ark

See how many plastic animals you can put into a pie pan ark before it sinks.

What You Need

- an aluminum foil pie pan

- a set of plastic animals (Use plastic clothespins if you don't have animals.)

What You Do

1. Put the pie pan in the water.

2. Add one animal at a time.
   Count as you add more.
   *How many animals can ride
   in the "ark" before it sinks?*

3. Try different small toys.

Shaving Like Daddy

Two-year-olds love to imitate the events they see around them.

What You Need

• soap foam—foam from tearless shampoo, suds from baby soap

What You Do

1. Put foam on your child's cheeks and chin.

2. Have him or her use a finger "razor" to shave it off.

Note: Tell your child that this is pretend.
Make sure that real razors are out of reach.

Take It Off

Two-year-olds are better at undressing than dressing.

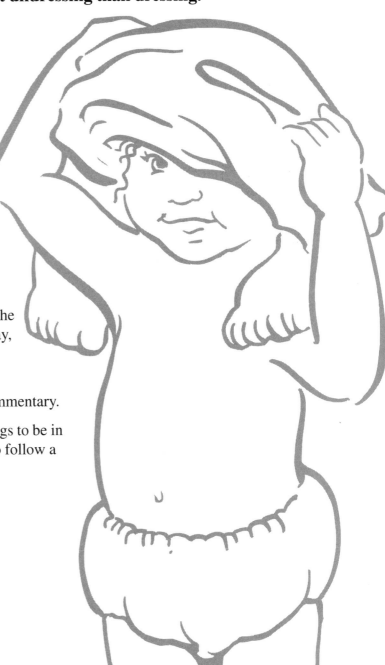

What You Need

- a fully clothed toddler
- clothes hamper

What You Do

While the tub is filling, have your child undress.

1. Name each article of clothing as it is removed.

2. Have your child put the clothing in the hamper or in its designated place. Say,
   Scotty's shirt is in the hamper.
   Scotty's shoes are on the shelf.

3. Soon your child will provide the commentary.

Because many two-year-olds want things to be in a certain order, undressing may need to follow a specific routine.

I Can Do It!

Help your child take an active part in getting dressed.

What You Need

- socks
- shirt
- pants

What You Do

Most two-year-olds are able to put on socks and sometimes a shirt or pants. Help extend their feeling of independence by showing them how to put clothes on and providing time for practice.

1. Begin with the socks.

2. Next a shirt...
   Try placing the shirt on the floor with the back facing up. Show your child how to put hands in the bottom opening and scoop the shirt over the head.

3. Finally, pants...
   Begin with pajama bottoms or sweatpants.
   Sit on the floor and put on one leg at a time.
   Grab the waist, stand up, and pull up the pants.

4. Praise your child's steps toward independence.

Mealtime

I like eating.
I like mixing.
Watch me. Watch me.
See me fixing.
Fixing dinner,
Fixing lunch –
I like fixing
A whole big bunch!

Play and Learn to

- practice fine-motor coordination
- develop sense of touch
- experience texture and shape
- improve ability to grasp
- taste new foods
- imitate actual experiences

Activities

I Can Help

Your two-year-old learns by imitating your everyday kitchen routine.

What You Need

- low cupboard or drawer

- an accessible work surface

- plastic measuring cups, plastic or wooden spoons, a plastic bowl, small saucepan, dishtowel, any utensils that are easily manipulated and safe

- a small scrubbing pad or brush

What You Do

1. Designate an area for storing your two-year-old's kitchen equipment.

2. Encourage your two-year-old to use the equipment to:

   - imitate your work in the kitchen
   - explore pouring and measuring
   - help prepare food for meals

Some jobs that two-year-olds can do include:

scrubbing—potatoes and carrots
tearing—lettuce into pieces
breaking—cauliflower or broccoli
shelling—peas
stirring—batter, fruit into yogurt, tuna salad
rinsing—fruit
cutting—cookies with cookie cutters

A Tub of Rice

Learn about full and empty by filling containers with rice.

What You Need

- a set of plastic measuring cups
- small plastic glasses
- measuring spoons
- a tub or large bowl
- rice

What You Do

1. Fill the tub with rice.

2. Give your child the containers.

3. Have your child fill the containers with rice.

4. After a period of filling and dumping exploration, direct the rice play by showing your child an empty cup and explaining,
   When a cup doesn't have anything in it, we say it's empty.

5. Show a full cup and explain,
   When a cup is filled to the top, we say it's full.

6. Then ask your child to show you a full container and an empty container.

> The rice tub can be used over and over. Keep a whisk broom and little dust pan with it for quick clean-up.

Use Your Senses

Screwing and unscrewing lids develops finger strength and coordination.

What You Need

- plastic containers with screw lids
- storage containers, water bottles

What You Do

1. Demonstrate how a screw lid works. Explain how to twist the lid while you hold the container in the other hand.

2. Next have your two-year-old hold the container. You do the twisting.

3. Then you hold the container and your two-year-old does the twisting.

4. Finally, your two-year-old takes over the whole job.

You may complete this progression in one session or over several months, depending on your child's interest and small-muscle development. Move to a more difficult level only as your child is ready.

Use the same "You hold, I'll twist" approach to pickle bottles, mustard and mayonnaise jars, and other screw-lid containers that you need to open as you prepare meals. Be sure to thank your helper for holding the container.

Pack a Snack

A nutritious between-meal snack is more fun when it's packed in a special container.

What You Need

- little snacks in bite-sized pieces
  Cheerios®
  cucumber slices
  soft-cooked carrot circles
  banana, peach, or pear slices
  small pieces of soft cheese
  cooked macaroni noodles

- small containers with lids

- lunch box or bag (This can be as simple as a paper bag with handles or it can be a small lunch box with a handle just like big brother or sister's.)

What You Do

1. Have your two-year-old help put the snacks in the containers.

2. Pack the snacks in the lunch bag.

3. Find a spot where the two of you can enjoy your treat.

The anticipation of fixing the snack and then choosing a place to eat it makes the snack taste better and creates a special quiet time for the two of you. Be sure to carry on a conversation as you eat.

Cookie Cutouts

Decorating cookies is fun to do. Eating your creations is a special bonus.

What You Need

- brown sugar cookie dough
- cookie cutters
- cookie decorations—raisins, small gumdrops, cherry halves
- rolling pin
- baking pan

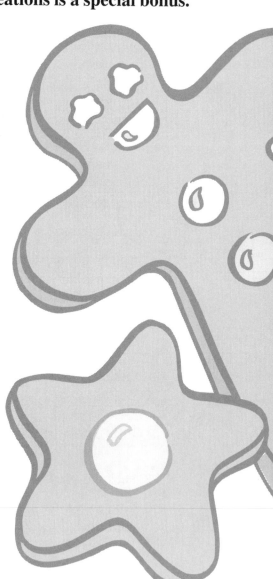

Brown Sugar Cookie Dough

Ingredients:
- 1 pound (454 g) of brown sugar
- 1 pound (455 g) of butter
- $4\frac{1}{2}$ cups (563 g) of flour
- 1 teaspoon (5 ml) of vanilla

What You Do

1. Prepare the dough.
   Cream butter, vanilla, and sugar.
   Add flour and mix well.
   Chill for at least one hour.

2. Sprinkle flour on the surface where you will roll the cookies.

3. Start with a small ball of dough and roll it flat.

4. Cut simple shapes with cookie cutters.

5. Move shapes to baking pan.

6. Add decorations.

7. Bake at 300º for 15 minutes.

Let your child participate as much as ability and interest allow. Be sure to explain what you are doing.

Wash the Dishes

Two-year-olds love to do what you're doing.

What You Need

- washtub with water and soap
- sponge or dishrag
- small plastic glasses and dishes

What You Do

1. If your child has a child-sized table or a low stool, put the tub of water on that surface. If you use a drain rack for drying, provide one for your child as well.

2. Stack small plastic dishes to be washed beside the tub and let your child take over.

3. Talk about what you're doing as you do it.

Sort Them and Put Them Away

The two-year-old's sense of order makes putting groceries away so natural!

What You Need

- bags of groceries
- sorting area

What You Do

1. Put grocery bags in the sorting area.

2. Work together to take the groceries out of the bags.

3. Then work together to put the groceries where they belong.

- Have your child sort a group of items for you to put away. Say,

  Can you put all the cans in a stack for me?

- Have your child put several similar items away.

  Please put all the boxes of Jell-O® away.

- Ask your child to locate an item and then put it away.

  Can you find the roll of paper towels and put it in the cupboard?

- Hand a familiar item to your child and ask him or her to put it where it belongs.

  Here's a box of Cheerios®. Please put it on the cereal shelf.

Show Me One, Show Me Two

Setting the table is a good time to practice beginning counting.

What You Need

- spoons

What You Do

As you set the table, play this spoon game with your two-year-old.

1. Put your two-year-old in a high chair.

2. Put several spoons on the tray.

3. Say,
   Give me one spoon for (family member's name).

4. Celebrate as one spoon is held up. Set the spoon at the appropriate spot on the table.

5. Repeat, asking for spoons for different family members until all the spoons are distributed.

6. Another time say,
   Give me two spoons for _____ and _____.

7. Finally, alternate *Give me one spoon* and *Give me two spoons.*

Indoor Playtime

Put it together.
Then take it apart.
It helps *me* to learn.
I'm getting so smart.

Play and Learn to

- develop sense of independence
- improve fine-motor coordination
- imitate actual experiences
- expand vocabulary
- build self-awareness and confidence
- follow simple directions

Activities

Notes on Safe Indoor Play with Two-Year-Olds

The success of your child's play indoors depends largely upon the presence of multiple, simple playthings and the absence of hazards. Carefully evaluate toys and objects in your child's environment for any hazards.

- Light plugs should be either disconnected or covered.
- Valuable or breakable objects should be removed from reach.
- Make sure furniture is sturdy.

- Install protective guards on sharp edges.
- Store toys on a low shelf where your child can reach them without climbing.
- Put medicines and cleaning supplies in a locked cabinet.

- Keep sharp utensils, plastic bags, and garbage out of reach.
- Outside doors should have locks or hooks that are out of reach.
- Stairways should have safety gates in place.

Play and Learn with Your Two-Year-Old • EMC 4501

Fingers + Paint

The sensation of thick, wet paint squishing between fingers is fun for two-year-olds and parents.

What You Need

- washable finger paint (buy at the store or make your own)
- oilcloth to paint on (buy at a fabric store)
- plastic drop cloth
- sponge and water for clean-up

What You Need

1. Cover a low table with a piece of oilcloth. Put a plastic drop cloth under the table to catch any drips.

2. Put several globs of finger paint on the oilcloth.

3. Show your two-year-old how to spread the paint with a hand.

4. Talk about how the paint feels as the two of you cover the oilcloth with your masterpiece.

5. Cleaning up is just as much fun as painting. Use a damp sponge to wipe the oilcloth clean. You're ready to start again.

A quick finger paint substitute: shaving cream foam

Homemade Finger Paint
Mix two cups of liquid starch, one cup of soap flakes, and water to make a thick, gooey paste. Add food coloring, if color is desired.

Playhouse

Playing house gives two-year-olds a chance to relive daily life.

What You Need

- an area designated as the house
- a doll or stuffed animal
- a hat or two
- a bed (see note below)
- an old baby blanket

What You Do

Your role in this dramatic play is directed by your child.

1. Provide the "playhouse" area and then wait for your child to begin.

2. Some two-year-olds will begin playing house by acting out bedtime routines. They put their dolls to bed, carefully covering them with blankets. Bedtime play sometimes includes changing diapers, reading books, singing songs, and rocking to sleep.

3. Other two-year-olds will enjoy "cooking and eating meals" or "going for a ride."

Note: Toy stores are full of child-sized equipment—doll beds, strollers, kitchen sets, tables and chairs. These props can add to dramatic play, but are not necessary. Your two-year-old may prefer to use a shoebox or a basket as a doll bed, rather than the expensive crib replica.

Puzzles

Put beginning puzzles together to practice perceptual skills.

What You Need

• a wooden puzzle with large pieces (the ones with knobs to hold on to are particularly good for two-year-olds)

What You Do

1. Sit on the floor next to your child. Lift one puzzle piece out of the puzzle. Then put it back to demonstrate how it fits to make the picture complete.

2. Have your child remove a puzzle piece and put it back in.

3. Progress to dumping the entire puzzle and putting it together. Let your child take the lead. Suggest solutions if he or she is stumped.

   Let's turn the piece around and see if it fits.
   What does this piece show? Where could it go?

4. Enjoy more difficult puzzles together as your child is ready.

My son, Mark, was much better at puzzles than me. He could dump and remake a puzzle in record time.

Take It Apart, Put It Together

Two-year-olds like to take things apart and put them back together.

What You Need

Provide some or all of the following:

- stacking toys
- toy flashlight
- cars or trains that can be taken apart and recombined
- puzzle blocks
- sipper bottle
- Duplo® blocks

Remember, expensive toys are not essential. Your two-year-old will enjoy taking an inexpensive sipper bottle apart and then putting it back together.

What You Do

1. Show the complete item and name it.
   This is my sipper bottle.

2. Explain that it comes apart.
   I can take it apart so that I can wash it or fill it.

3. Take it apart.
   This is the lid. This is the straw. This is the bottle.

4. Then put the bottle back together. Make several take-apart, put-together items available.

Counting Songs

Make up and sing songs to count objects around your home.

What You Need

• a group of objects

What You Do

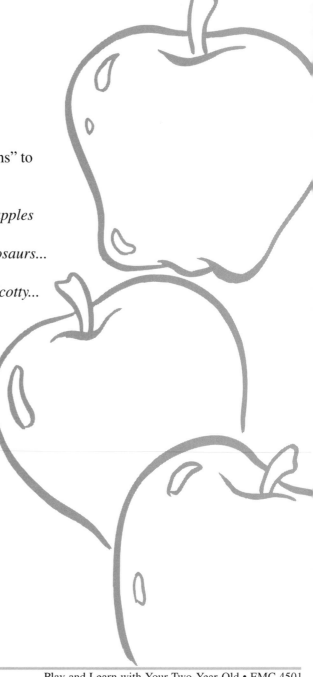

1. Sing an original version of "Ten Little Indians" to count a group of objects.

   For unpacking the groceries,
   > *one-little, two-little, big green apples*

   For picking up toys,
   > *one-little, two-little, purple dinosaurs...*

   For folding laundry,
   > *one-little, two-little, shirts for Scotty...*

2. Have your child pick up the objects as you count.

Don't be surprised to hear the same songs during your child's playhouse time.

Playclay Play

**Roll it and prick it and mark it with a P.
Playclay play is easy as can be!**

What You Need

• playclay (Buy it at the store or make your own using the recipe on page 30.)

• a tray or flat surface for sculpting

What You Do

1. Enjoy the clay. You might:
   • Pick up a handful and squeeze it out through your fingers.

   • Roll a ball between your hands.

   • Flatten a ball.

   • Make big balls and little balls.

   • Create a new shape.

2. As you and your child play, talk about what you're doing.
   I'm making a ball. See how I roll the playclay between my hands.
   I put my ball on the table and push on it.
   Now it looks like a pancake.

3. Ask questions.
   What are you making?
   How did you make that little ball?

4. Make size comparisons.
   Your hill is taller than my hill.
   Can you make me a bigger hill?

Playclay Recipe

Ingredients:
  3 cups (375 g) of flour
  1 cup (288 g) of salt
  1 cup (240 ml) of water
  ¼ cup (60 ml) of cooking oil
  2 tablespoons (30 ml) of vinegar

1. Mix the ingredients in a bowl.

2. Add more water if needed to make the clay pliable.

3. Knead the clay until soft.

4. Store in a plastic bag.

Hint: When the clay becomes stiff and flaky, add a little water and knead it in.

Frosting Dough

Here is another tactile experience that's fun and edible.

What You Need

- frosting dough (recipe on page 32)
- a tray or flat surface for sculpting
- spoon
- bowl
- measuring cup

What You Do

1. Mix the dough together.
2. Enjoy squeezing and molding.
3. If you want a sweet treat, mold a tiny animal and pop it in your mouth.

Frosting Dough

Ingredients:
  can of ready-made frosting
  1½ cups (185 g) of powdered sugar
  1 cup (224 g) of peanut butter

1. Mix all the ingredients in a bowl with the spoon.
2. Knead the dough until it is workable.

Build It with Blocks

Stack blocks to make towers. Then knock them down.

What You Need

• a set of blocks

Wooden blocks should be smooth. All blocks should be big enough so that they can't be put in the mouth, but small enough to be easily picked up and moved.

What You Do

1. Sit with your child on the floor.

2. Let your child explore using the blocks.

3. Suggest building a tower. Take turns stacking the blocks. Enjoy the crash when it collapses.

4. Continue as long as building and knocking down are fun for your child. If he or she prefers to simply line up the blocks or build independently, sit nearby and enjoy the experience.

Collect the Clothespins

Sharpen perceptual skills with this homemade toy.

What You Need

- half-gallon plastic juice container with a narrow mouth
- wooden clothespins
- permanent markers

What You Do

1. Use permanent markers to draw different faces and hats on the clothespins.

2. Have your child put the clothespins in the mouth of the juice container.

3. When all the pins are in, shake the container to dump them out.

4. Tell your child which pin to put in the bottle.
   Put the man with the blue hat in the bottle.

Outdoor Playtime

I sit on the seat.
I push with my feet.
Ready, set, go!
I'll put on a show.

Play and Learn to

- practice climbing and descending
- improve perceptual skills
- develop sense of balance
- improve large-motor skills
- satisfy curiosity
- identify opposites
- sharpen conceptual thinking
- exercise perceptions of space and distance
- imitate actual experiences

Activities

Notes on Safe Outdoor Play with Two-Year-Olds

Just as in indoor play, the success of your child's play outdoors depends largely upon the presence of multiple, simple playthings and the absence of any hazards. It is up to you to evaluate your child's environment for any hazards.

Outdoor play with two-year-olds should be loosely structured. Children should move freely. Parents interact by playing beside their children, talking, listening, observing, and keeping the activity safe.

• Install locks high on fence gates.

• Store all gardening tools and supplies in a locked shed.

• Get rid of plants and shrubs with poisonous leaves or berries. Set up play equipment on grass or sand, not on a hard surface.

• Cover the sandbox when it's not in use.

• Never leave your child unattended.

• Think about sunburns before they happen.

Carry Me Home

Always take a wagon or a stroller along as you explore new places or do your errands.

What You Need

• a wagon or a stroller

What You Do

1. Start off with your two-year-old pulling a wagon or walking beside you as you pull the wagon. An empty wagon? No way! Put an old towel in the bottom of the wagon. Be sure to include a water bottle and a snack. Your child may want to bring a favorite stuffed animal along for the ride.

2. Adjust your pace to your child's. Point out things as you pass. Enjoy the stroll.

3. Don't be surprised if your little one's legs give out before you get home. Simply load him or her in the wagon and continue home.

Push It Over Here

It's fun to put something in a wheelbarrow and push it from one place to another.

What You Need

- a small wheelbarrow or a tiny pull-box you have created using PVC pipe scraps, duct tape, and a cardboard box

Note: Your child will pull the pull-box rather than push it.

What You Do

1. Add a wheelbarrow to your child's outdoor play area.

2. Give a ride to a stuffed friend or a sand pail to demonstrate how the wheelbarrow works.

3. As you do yard work with your regular wheelbarrow, involve your child on a smaller scale. Your child can haul small loads with his or her wheelbarrow.

Imitating everyday routines outside is just as important as imitating them inside.

Water Painting

Your child will love painting walls, fences, and outdoor furniture.

What You Need

- a small tub
- a small paint roller

What You Do

1. Fill the tub with water.
2. Dip the roller in the water and show how the roller is used to spread the water.
3. Give the roller to your child.

If you have items that can't get wet, move them before beginning this project.

Watering Day

Your two-year-old will love watering with the hose.

What You Need

- a hose
- a nozzle for adjusting the spray

What You Do

1. Set up the hose in a place where water will not do any damage.

2. Let your child water plants, grass, bushes, shrubs, and areas of your garden.

Don't expect your two-year-old to take over the responsibility of actually watering the plants or grass. Think of this activity as water play, not work.

My grandson, Josh, loves to water my yard. He always says, "I'll be the rain."

Sand Play

Filling a pan or a bucket with sand and then dumping it can occupy hours.

What You Need

- small bucket
- plastic shovels
- cups, trucks, spoons
- a sandbox or pile of loose dirt

What You Do

1. Simply provide the equipment.
2. Join in the fun!

Some variations for sandbox play:

- On a hot day sprinkle the sand with water.
- Dig trenches and lakes and fill them with water.
- Set up a digging station near a pile of dirt. Instead of sand, play with mud.

> Your child may not be interested in building a particular structure. It is the filling, carrying, dumping, and refilling that become the main activities.

Throwing and Catching

Throw and catch beanbags and foam balls.

What You Need

• beanbag, foam ball

What You Do

1. Stand about three feet in front of your child.

2. Your child forms a hand nest.

3. Gently toss the beanbag into the nest.

4. Child closes hands around the beanbag.

5. Child throws beanbag back to you.

Repeat as long as this is fun for your child or until you collapse! Gradually extend the distance between the two of you.

Walk the Curb

Practice balance by walking along your driveway curb.

What You Need

- a low curb in a safe place

What You Do

1. Show your child how to walk along a curb, putting one foot directly in front of the other.

2. Hold one hand to provide security as your child tries the balance walk.

3. Celebrate success.

When your child is ready, encourage independence.

Big, Small, Soft, Loud

Note opposites as you play and learn outside.

What You Need

• the things around you

What You Do

Use any opportunity to encourage your child's use of language. Observe and point out opposites as you use all of your senses outside:

1. Sit quietly and listen for different sounds. Comment on the sounds you hear. Encourage your child to connect sounds with their source.

   P.J.'s bark is a loud sound.
   Holly's meow is a soft sound.
   Tell me about the sounds you hear.

2. Lie on your backs and look up at the sky.

   Look at that big cloud.
   There's a small cloud over there.

3. Feel the grass with your bare toes. Then walk on the sidewalk.

   The grass feels prickly and soft.
   The cement is hard and smooth.

Riding Toys

Two-year-olds use their legs together to propel themselves forward on low-wheeled vehicles.

What You Need

- a large area with a hard surface

- a wheeled vehicle without pedals

Note: Make sure that the area you are using is safe. Your child will not be able, at first, to stop quickly or to judge distances, so you must think in advance to prevent accidents. Be especially alert for sloping areas that lead into a street and decks or driveways with drop-offs.

What You Do

1. Enjoy your child's play.

2. Encourage awareness of space by having your child follow simple directions.

   Ride over to that side of the driveway and come back.

   Drive your truck to the swing and back again.

Play and Learn with Your Two-Year-Old • EMC 4501

Eating Outside

Enjoy the freedom of a picnic whether you sit at a picnic table, on an old throw rug, or in your car.

What You Need

- a container to carry your food
- food
- water or juice
- something to sit on (optional)

What You Do

Picnics are fun for parents as well as children.

1. Pack several of your child's favorite finger foods; a large, soft blanket; a bucket and a toy shovel; and plenty of liquids. You may take your picnic to a special destination, but going somewhere is not necessary. Your child will enjoy the picnic on your front step, in your backyard, or on your kitchen floor.

2. Spread out the feast and enjoy. Don't forget to carry on a picnic conversation.

You'll find recipes for some good picnic foods my children enjoyed as two-year-olds on pages 47 and 48. Remember to let your child share in the preparation of the food.

Fruit on a Stick

- melon cubes
- pineapple chunks
- strawberries

Use any of your child's favorite fruits cut in small pieces.

Stick several pieces of fruit on a plastic stirrer.

Fruit Dip

Combine yogurt and honey to taste. (Start with a teaspoon (7 g) of honey to $1/3$ of a small carton of yogurt.) Store in a small, covered container. Dip the fruit in and then eat.

Picnic Cookies

Ingredients:
- 1 cup (192 g) of shortening
- 1 cup (220 g) of brown sugar
- 1 cup (200 g) of granulated sugar
- 2 eggs
- 1 teaspoon (5 ml) of vanilla
- 1½ cups (185 g) of flour
- 1 teaspoon (4 g) of soda
- 3 cups (240 g) of quick-cooking rolled oats
- 8-ounce package (226 g) of butterscotch chips

1. To make dough:
   Cream shortening and sugars.
   Add eggs and vanilla.
   Beat well.
   Add flour and soda to creamed mixture.
   Stir in rolled oats. Add chips.
   Mix.

2. Form dough into 3 rolls about 2 inches in diameter.

3. Wrap in plastic wrap. Store in freezer.

4. When you want warm cookies:
   Slice ¼" rounds from frozen cookie roll.
   Bake on ungreased cookie sheet at
   350˚ (175º C) for 8–10 minutes.

Bedtime

Say good night to Cat and Ted.
Plump the pillow for my head.
Tuck me in for my nightly book.
Hold the pages so I can look.
Read every word. (I'll make sure you do.)
Now a kiss and a bear hug, too.
Please, some water. Rub my back.
Could I be an insomniac?

Play and Learn to

- increase phonemic awareness
- develop memory and vocabulary
- improve ability to concentrate
- learn about rhythm
- follow simple directions
- feel loved and safe

Activities

Action Rhymes

Chant and sing simple rhyming verses as you clap and do simple actions.

What You Need

• a rhyme in your head (see pages 51 and 52)

What You Do

When you first introduce an action rhyme, do it for your child several times.

1. Sit your child on your lap facing you.

2. Repeat the rhyme with actions. Soon your child will imitate your actions.

3. Applaud the attempts. Celebrate each performance.

Learn the four rhymes on the next two pages. Use them anytime during the day when you have a quiet moment.

The Birthday Cake

Two candles on a birthday cake.
All lit up for me.
I'll make a wish and blow them out.
Watch and you will see.

Patty Cake

Patty cake, patty cake, baker's man.
Bake me a cake as fast as you can.
Roll it and prick it and mark it with B.
Put it in the oven for baby and me.

Blowing Balloons

This is the way
We blow a balloon.
Blow. Blow. Blow.
This is the way
We break a balloon.
Oh, oh, no!

Apples in My Tree

Way up high in the apple tree,
Two little apples smiled at me.
I shook that tree as hard as I could.
Down came the apples—
Mmmm, were they good!

Play and Learn with Your Two-Year-Old • EMC 4501

Bounce and Rhyme

Your child will enjoy bouncing to these traditional lap rhymes and songs.

What You Need

- a lap

- strong legs

- a rhyme in your head (see pages 54 and 55)

What You Do

1. Sit your child on your lap facing you with one leg on either side of your legs as if riding a horse.

2. Bounce your child in rhythm as you repeat the rhyme.

3. Listen to the words and "bounce" accordingly. In "Trotty Horse," open your legs and let your child "fall" through. In "The Grand Old Duke of York," lean your child left, then right, then turn him or her upside down.

(Keep a firm hold of the child's hands as you tip him or her backwards.)

bedtime • bedtime • bedtime • bedtime • bedtime • bedtime • bedtime • bedtime • bedtime • bedtime • bedtime • bedtime • bedtime • bedti

Ride a Cockhorse

Ride a cockhorse to Banbury Cross,
To see a fine lady upon a white horse.
Rings on her fingers and bells on her toes,
She shall have music wherever she goes.

Trotty Horse

Trotty horse, trotty horse to the mill
To see Grandpappy and Uncle Bill.
Trotty horse, trotty horse to the town.
Watch out, little (child's name), don't you fall down!

The Grand Old Duke of York

The Grand Old Duke of York,
He had ten thousand men.
He marched them up to the top of the hill,
And he marched them down again.

And when they were up, they were up.
And when they were down, they were down.
And when they were only halfway up,
They were neither up nor down.

You can lean them to the left.
You can lean them to the right.
And when you turn them
upside down,
Oh, what a silly sight!

Picking Up

Involve your child in picking up nightly before bed.

What You Need

• a basket for soiled clothing

• low shelving for blocks and toys

What You Do

Give simple directions as you share the responsibilities for picking up. Give the directions using face-saving strategies. Try not to trap yourself in some inflexible demand or power struggle.

Let's put your socks in the basket and your shoes on the shelf.

Where do your clothes go?

We'll read our book just as soon as we have put the toys on the shelf.

You may have to do the major part of the work yourself, but you have involved your child in the idea of cleaning up and have bypassed a possible confrontation. Don't expect a two-year-old to pick up a room all alone, but do expect some participation.

My Bedtime List

Create a checklist to support your child's bedtime routine.

What You Need

- paper and markers

What You Do

1. As your two-year-old develops a routine for bedtime, record the steps on a simple chart.
   - Write one or two words.
   - Draw a picture to represent the word(s).

2. Post the chart on a door. Refer to the chart at bedtime.

3. You and your child can read the chart together. You might ask your child to:
   - identify the pictures.
     Show me the bathtub.
     Where's the toothbrush?
   - tell what comes next.
     We brush your teeth.
     What should we do next?

The chart may make it easier for sitters to follow the routine. It will help your child understand that words have meaning. Don't expect two-year-olds to read the words. They should simply recognize that they are words.

While-You-Wait Time

Waiting is quite hard to do.
It's hard on me
And it's hard on you.
I'll try to be patient,
Yes, I will,
If you keep talking
And don't stand still.

Play and Learn to

- practice perceptual skills
- develop self-awareness and confidence
- sharpen memory and coordination
- develop vocabulary
- learn about qualities and characteristics
- improve dexterity

Activities

Look All Around

Think of waiting as an opportunity to learn about new things.

What You Need

• the things around you

What You Do

1. As you wait in line or in a waiting room, point out the things around you.

2. In simple language explain the name of the object, what it does, and how it affects your child.

> *Look. There's a special camera that takes our picture while we wait in line here at the bank. It helps the bank to know who comes in each day.*

Two-year-olds may especially enjoy:
• machines
   computers, check-out registers, surveillance cameras
• animals
   fish in a tank, birds outside the window, seeing-eye dog
• other babies and children
• vehicles of all kinds

Where Is It?

Practice memory and sensory awareness with this simple game.

What You Need

- several objects—items out of your purse or backpack such as a key ring, a comb, a case for glasses

- a blanket or a sweater or jacket

What You Do

1. Show your child one object.

2. Put the object under a blanket.

3. Then ask,
   Where is (the object)?

4. The child should point to the bump or remove the blanket to show the object.

5. When your child seems confident with one object, try two.

   - Show the two objects.
   - Put them under the blanket.
   - Ask,
     Which one is the (object)?

   Your child will have to use the shape of the bump under the blanket to identify the object.

6. Have your child hide an object.

What Can It Do?

Connect your child's experiences with magazine illustrations as the two of you talk about what animals can do.

What You Need

• pictures of animals
(Use the magazines in the waiting room or the placards on the wall of the bus.)

What You Do

1. Say the name of an animal or show the animal's picture.

2. Ask,
   What can a (animal name) do?

3. Your child may answer with the sound the animal makes, a single word, or a recounting of a remembered experience.
   What can a dog do?
   Woof-Woof. Doggie go. Doggie lick Sam.

At first, point out only animals that your child knows.
Later, point out new animals and give information as needed.
   What can a llama do?
   A llama can carry heavy things to help people.

Show Me!

Stuck at a meeting or an appointment without a toy?
Play this simple identification game.

What You Need

• your child

What You Do

1. Say,
   Show me a hand.

2. Your child holds up a hand.

3. Continue with other body parts, pieces of clothing, or items in the waiting room.

4. Move on to simple actions.
   Show me a jump.

While-We-Wait Handkerchief

A handkerchief or a simple facial tissue doubles as a great diversion.

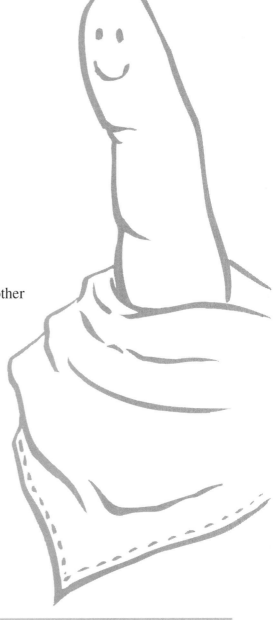

What You Need

- a handkerchief

What You Do

Keep your handkerchief with you in a pocket or purse. Be ready to use it for these "time passers":

Handkerchief Puppet

1. Put your index finger straight up.

2. Put the handkerchief around the finger.

3. Carefully grasp the tails of the handkerchief with your other fingers, leaving your index finger extended.

4. Move your finger and talk. You may even want to add eyes and a mouth with your pen.
   Where are my eyes? Hey, can anybody see me? I need some eyes.

Handkerchief Hide and Seek

1. Put the handkerchief partially into a pocket or sleeve.

2. Ask,
   Where is the handkerchief?

3. Continue hiding the handkerchief in increasingly difficult places.

Travel Time

Think ahead.
Plan well in advance.
Don't leave traveling
just to chance.

- experience texture and shape

- improve ability to grasp
  and squeeze

- develop fine-motor
  coordination

- improve memory and
  coordination

- learn about rhythm

- develop phonemic awareness

Activities

Activities-to-Go

Pack a basket or box with travel activities for your car.

What You Need

- a basket or box
- lidded container filled with small plastic animals
- soft doll or animal (one with buttons and zippers keeps little hands busy)
- board book
- other things as desired

What You Do

1. Work together with your child to select and pack the items for your travel basket.

2. Help your child carry the basket to your car and find a place to store it. (It's best if it can be reached from the car seat.)

3. Preparing the basket in advance will save you time and make getting ready to go somewhere much easier.

4. Add new surprises to the basket occasionally.

Fishing for a Toy

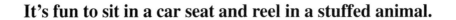

It's fun to sit in a car seat and reel in a stuffed animal.

What You Need

- a small stuffed animal
- a long scarf

What You Do

1. Tie one end of the scarf to the front of the car seat.

2. Tie the other end of the scarf to the stuffed animal.

3. Give the animal to your child.

4. When your child is tired of playing with the animal and drops it…

5. Show how to pull on the scarf to retrieve the animal. A new game—Drop It and Reel It In—will begin.

Sing Along

Singing together is a great way to develop phonemic awareness.

What You Need

- songs in your head (Try the ones on pages 68 and 69.)
- a tape player and tapes (optional)

What You Do

1. Sing the old favorites you remember from your childhood or learn a few new tunes. Don't worry about getting the words or the tune perfect. Just enjoy. Start with nursery rhymes and move on to those wonderful multiverse tales that go on forever, such as *Old MacDonald Had a Farm* or *This Old Man*.

2. After your child becomes familiar with the words, stop singing just before the final word, so he or she can finish the line.

As I drove across Kansas taking my daughter to college, she and her brother sang all the songs that they remembered from car trips when they were little. You should have seen them singing Gary LaPou's *Noodle Song* with all the hand motions we had made up many years ago.

Hickory Dickory Dock

Hickory dickory dock,
The mouse ran up the clock.
The clock struck one,
And down he run.
Hickory dickory dock.

Twinkle, Twinkle, Little Star

Twinkle, twinkle, little star,
How I wonder what you are.
Up above the world so high,
Like a diamond in the sky.
Twinkle, twinkle, little star,
How I wonder what you are.

Mary Had a Little Lamb

Mary had a little lamb, little lamb, little lamb
Mary had a little lamb with fleece as white as snow.
Everywhere that Mary went, Mary went, Mary went
Everywhere that Mary went, the lamb was sure to go.
It followed her to school one day, school one day, school one day
It followed her to school one day which was against the rule.
It made the children laugh and play, laugh and play, laugh and play.
It made the children laugh and play to see a lamb at school.

Old MacDonald Had a Farm

Old MacDonald had a farm, E-I-E-I-O.
And on this farm he had some chicks, E-I-E-I-O.
With a chick-chick here,
And a chick-chick there,
Here a chick,
There a chick,
Everywhere a chick-chick.
Old MacDonald had a farm, E-I-E-I-O.

Add animals and animal noises until you can't think of anymore!

Make It Fit

Your child will learn about shapes as he or she puts things in a shape sorter.

What You Need

• a purchased sorter such as Tupperware®
  Shape Ball or a homemade sorter

film canister	curler
block	raisin box
shoe box or other small, sturdy box	

To Make the Homemade Sorter

1. Trace a circle the diameter of the film canister on the top of the shoebox.

2. Trace a square the size of the block on top of the box.

3. Cut out the circle and the square.

Make sure that the curler and the raisin box also fit through the holes you've made. Adjust holes as needed.

What You Do

1. Give your child the four objects and the box.

2. Have your child put the objects in the box.

3. Add other household objects to your shape collection. This search becomes another play-and-learn activity.

4. Ask,

    What can we find in the kitchen that will fit in this hole?

Be sure that the objects you find are too big to go in your child's mouth and do not have sharp edges.

Nuts and Bolts

Twist and turn nuts on a big bolt to practice coordination.

What You Need

- a long, lightweight bolt
- several washers and nuts of different sizes that fit on the bolt
- Super Glue®

What You Do

1. Put the washers and nuts on the bolt.

2. Glue the last nut at the end of the bolt with Super Glue® to prevent the removal of the other pieces.

3. Let it dry and check to make sure that the glued nut is secure.

4. Give the bolt to your child and show how the nuts and washers can be twisted and moved from one end to the other.

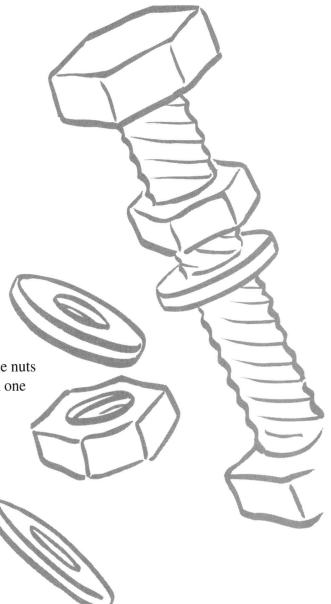

Nesting Boxes

It's fun to discover a surprise in this nest of boxes.

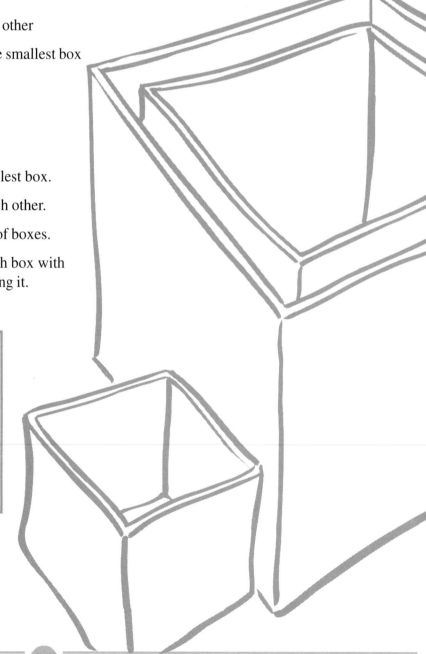

What You Need

- 3 boxes that fit inside each other
- an object that fits inside the smallest box

What You Do

1. Put the object in the smallest box.

2. Nest the boxes inside each other.

3. Give your child the nest of boxes.

For a special treat, wrap each box with wrapping paper before nesting it.

Just before Mother's Day, I carefully wrapped gifts for each of two-year-old Mark's grandmothers. I explained to him that we would send the gifts in the mail. I walked into the kitchen to get a box. When I came back moments later, Mark had unwrapped each of the gifts. He sat happily amidst the torn wrappings.

Story Time

I like to snuggle on your lap
And read a book before my nap.

Play and Learn to

- identify details in pictures
- hear rhythm and rhyme to develop phonemic awareness
- repeat words and sounds to extend vocabulary
- identify shapes and colors
- sharpen conceptual thinking
- develop memory

Activities

Shared Reading

Sit your child on your lap or snuggle together and share a favorite book. Continue to develop the good reading practices that you began with your one-year-old. Reading is ageless.

One of the joys of sharing books and stories with young children is watching their reactions to the same book change as they grow and mature. The simple text and bold drawings in *Brown Bear, Brown Bear* by Bill Martin, Jr. is a favorite among young listeners.

- At first, babies will enjoy hearing the rhythm of the words as the pages turn.

- A bit later, they'll start to learn the names of the animals and the sounds that they make.

- Soon they'll start turning the pages and calling out the animal on the next page before they even see it.

What You Need

- Good books!
  Find sturdy board books with clear shapes and colors, plus a variety of picture books with limited text.

What You Do

1. At first, choose wordless books or books with only names or labels. Turn the pages and point out the objects in the illustrations. Relate the objects to your child's experiences.
   - Use your child's name.
     Look at the bear. Is it Josh's teddy?
   - Talk about your child's favorite activities.
     See the little girl in the book. She's taking a bath.
     You just took a bath, too.

2. Read from a collection of Mother Goose rhymes. The rhythm and the rhyme of the text will engage your two-year-old.

3. Choose books with repetition and pattern in the words and story structure.

4. Choose high-interest topics like bath and bedtime, toys, and animals.

A few suggestions:

Bookstores and libraries are filled with wonderful books for you and your child to share. There are a number of excellent read-aloud guides that will help you choose good literature appropriate to the age of your child.

Buy a few special books to enjoy over and over again at bedtime. Be sure to consider these books, just a few of my favorites:

Moo, Baa, La La La by Sandra Boynton; Simon & Schuster, 1982.

Go, Dog, Go!: P.D. Eastman's Book of Things That Go by P.D. Eastman; Random House, 1997.

Green Eggs and Ham by Dr. Seuss; Random House, 1960.

Chicka Chicka Boom Boom by Bill Martin, Jr. and John Archambault; Simon & Schuster, 1989.

From Head to Toe by Eric Carle; Harper Collins, 1997.

Sam's Wagon by Barbro Lindgren; William Morrow, 1986.

Snowballs by Lois Ehlert; Harcourt Brace & Company, 1995.

Time To Sleep by Denise Fleming; Henry Holt, 1997.

Where's Spot? by Eric Hill; Putnam, 1990.

One of the most important things you can do to encourage a love of reading is to read to your child early.

Tell a Teddy

Tell a story to your child's bear as your child listens and plays nearby.

What You Need

- a story
- a bear

What You Do

1. Sit down near the place your child is playing.

2. Perch your child's teddy bear on your lap and tell a story.

Try a true story about your child or a traditional favorite like *The Three Little Pigs*.

Puppets

Some two-year-olds love puppets. Use a puppet to tell a story.

What You Need

- a puppet—buy ready-made ones or make your own (see page 78)

What You Do

1. Put a puppet on your hand.

2. Start talking as the puppet.

Hi, Thomas. I'm Mr. Spoon. I want to tell you a story I know about Goldilocks and the Three Bears. It's all about some bears...

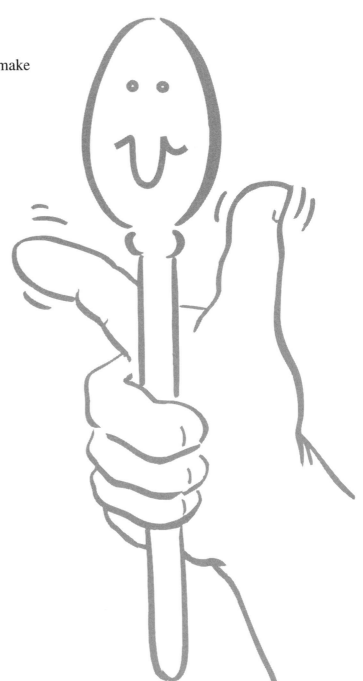

©1999 Evan-Moor Corp.

Play and Learn with Your Two-Year-Old • EMC 4501

Tube Sock Pop-Up

What You Need

- tube sock
- small empty Pringles® canister or small plastic flower pot
- chopstick
- stuffing (a plastic grocery bag cut into strips)
- pens
- double-sided tape

What You Do

1. Stuff the toe of the sock.

2. Hold stuffing in place with a rubber band. This makes the puppet's head.

3. Make a hole in the bottom of the empty canister.

4. Push the chopstick through the hole and into the stuffed head.

5. Stretch the sock over the outside of the canister and fasten with double-sided tape.

6. Draw eyes and mouth with marking pens.

7. Add hair and hat if desired.

8. Move head up and down to play peek-a-boo.

A Book about Me

Make a simple scrapbook with photos of your child's favorite things.

What You Need

- a scrapbook with several sturdy pages
- photos of your child

What You Do

1. Put a single photo of your child on each page. It's not necessary to label or write captions, but you may if you want.

2. Share the book with your child often.

   Here is a picture of you with Pony. You learned to walk pushing Pony down the hall.

   Look, here is Mr. Bear. Do you remember when we lost him at the mall?

A Refrigerator Gallery

Place current photographs of you and your child on the refrigerator and use them as the basis for your storytelling.

What You Need

- current photos
- magnets

What You Do

1. Using magnets, place copies of photographs on the refrigerator at your child's eye level. Put the photos in a protective sleeve if you don't want fingerprints on them.

2. When you and your child are in the kitchen together, talk about the photos.
    - Prompt your child to tell about what is happening in the photo.
        Who is that?
        What is he/she doing?
        Why is he/she doing that?

    - Tell about the special occasion that prompted the photo.
        Remember when Uncle Steve came over for your birthday party? We had so much fun watching you unwrap the packages. You cried when Steve blew out the candles on your cake. Then you stuck your whole hand in the frosting.